GENETIC CONDITIONS

Hemophilia

RANDALL MCPARTLAND

Cavendish
Square

New York

Published in 2016 by Cavendish Square Publishing, LLC
243 5th Avenue, Suite 136, New York, NY 10016

Library of Congress Cataloging-in-Publication Data

McPartland, Randall, author.
Hemophilia / Randall McPartland.
pages cm. — (Genetic conditions)
Includes bibliographical references and index.
ISBN 978-1-5026-0944-1 (hardcover) ISBN 978-1-5026-0945-8 (ebook)
1. Hemophilia I. Title.
RC642.M39 2016
616.1'572—dc23

2015023057

Editorial Director: David McNamara
Editor: Fletcher Doyle
Copy Editor: Nathan Heidelberger
Art Director: Jeffrey Talbot
Designer: Alan Sliwinski
Senior Production Manager: Jennifer Ryder-Talbot
Production Editor: Renni Johnson
Photo Research: J8 Media

The photographs in this book are used by permission and through the courtesy of: Cultura/
Jason Butcher/Getty Images, cover; FreeBirdPhotos/Shutterstock.com, 5; ChameleonsEye/
Shutterstock.com, 8; Alila Medical Media/Shutterstock.com, 9; Designua/Shutterstock.
com, 12; Zuzanae/Shutterstock.com, 15; Popperfoto/Getty Images, 18; Hulton Archive/Getty
Images, 20; Wellcome Images/File:Albucasis blistering a patient in the hospital at Cordova.
Wellcome V0018145.jpg/Wikimedia Commons, 22; New York Public Library/Getty Images,
24; Courtesy of Kristy Dobson, 27; Biophoto Associates/Getty Images, 28; Kim Komenich/
The LIFE Images Collection/Getty Images, 30; Blausen.com staff/File:Blausen 0181 Catheter
CentralVenousAccessDevice NonTunneled.png/Wikimedia Commons, 35; Jan Arkesteijn/
File:James D Watson.jpg/Wikimedia Commons, 38; Joel Rennich UPI Photo Service/Newscom,
41; Steve Liss/The LIFE Images Collection/Getty Images, 43; Raphael GAILLARDE/Gamma-
Rapho via Getty Images, 49; PatrickMcMullan.com via AP Images, 51; AP Photo/University of
Georgia, Paul Efland, 54.

Printed in the United States of America

Contents

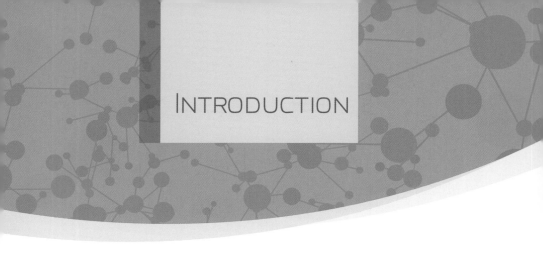

Hemophilia can be a frightening condition. Every physical activity brings with it the potential for a bruise or an injury that won't stop bleeding. Any cut must be taken care of immediately, and danger lurks everywhere.

When someone has hemophilia, his or her blood doesn't clot normally. It can take a long time to stop the flow of blood. Injuries that are not normally serious for most people can be life-threatening for people who suffer from hemophilia.

Hemophilia is a genetic disease. It is caused by a defect, or mistake, in one **gene**. Genes are the elements in our cells that carry the information that determines what traits we have, such as hair or eye color. In the case of hemophilia, there is a defect in the gene that controls the production of one of the thirteen substances, or **clotting factors**, that cause blood to clot. This defect can be passed on from parents to their children. It is something that a person is born with—it cannot be caught or contracted later in life.

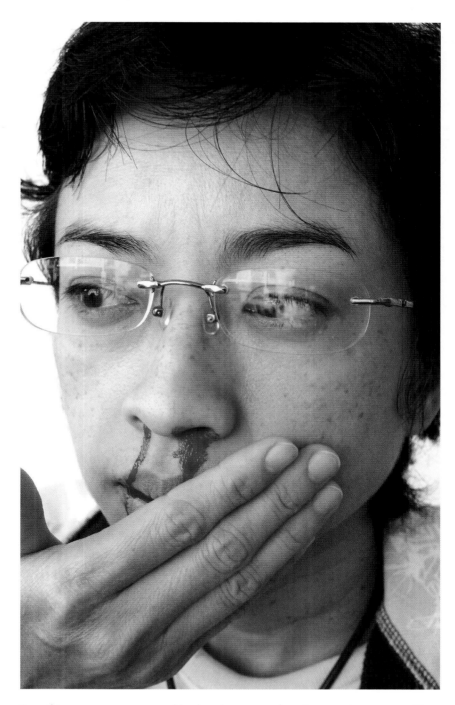

Something as common as a nosebleed can be a cause of great concern to someone with hemophilia or another bleeding disorder.

What is it like to have hemophilia? A person with a bleeding disorder must always be alert for cuts and bruises on his or her body. That person is unable to take part in some sports, such as hockey or football, although golf and swimming are relatively safe. When a hemophiliac notices that he or she is bleeding, treatment of the injury must start immediately. Especially troubling are bruises, which can indicate internal bleeding. If internal bleeding is not stopped, it can be very serious or even fatal. When bleeding needs to be stopped, the victim or a helper mixes the required medicine.

Sometimes other students at school pick on young hemophiliacs because they are different—the condition is rare. Sometimes people with the condition feel angry and frustrated that they have to deal with so many extra challenges. However, people with the condition are not alone. It is estimated that about twenty thousand Americans are living with the disease. The National Hemophilia Foundation estimates that there are more than four hundred thousand people worldwide with hemophilia.

This book exams the nature and history of hemophilia, and takes a look at research aimed at making the world less scary for a person with a bleeding disorder.

Bleeding Disorder

ircumcision is practiced by members of two of the world's largest religions, Islam and Judaism. Both trace the procedure back to Abraham, nearly four thousand years ago. According to the *Jewish Encyclopedia*, it was "enjoined upon Abraham and his descendants as 'a token of the covenant' concluded with him by God for all generations."

Since then, all Jewish males have been required to undergo the procedure (removal of the foreskin of the penis) eight days after they are born. However, the Talmud—rabbinic teachings on Jewish law—records exceptions to this rule.

Around 100 CE, **Rabbi** Judah the Patriarch stated that a baby boy may not undergo circumcision if he had a brother who had died of bleeding after this procedure.

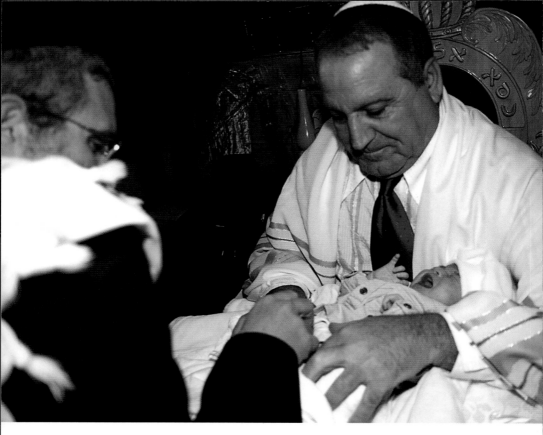

Circumcision has been performed on eight-day-old Jewish males for thousands of years.

One thousand years later, this ruling was extended by Moses Maimonides, a rabbi and lawmaker who lived in Egypt. He stated that if a woman married a second time, her sons by this second marriage should also be exempt from circumcision if any of her sons by her first marriage had suffered bleeding problems as a result of the procedure. These rulings showed that even back then people had a sense that certain disorders could be inherited, even if they did not understand exactly how the process worked. Today, any boy diagnosed with hemophilia is exempted from circumcision.

Hemophilia is caused by a problem with one of the substances in our blood that makes it clot. Blood clotting is a sequence of chemical activities. When a wound occurs in a blood vessel, blood cells called **platelets** clump together to start plugging the hole. This process is referred to as platelet adhesion. The first platelets to arrive at the damaged area put out chemicals that attract **proteins** called clotting factors. There are thirteen clotting factors, and they are labeled with Roman numerals I through XIII.

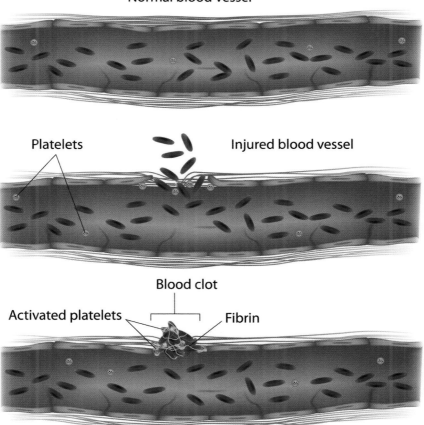

Normal blood vessel

Platelets   **Injured blood vessel**

Blood clot

Activated platelets   Fibrin

When a blood vessel is injured, hemostasis begins and platelets are activated. They are bound to the vessel wall and each other by von Willebrand factor. The platelets interact with other factors to help the blood clot and to create fibrin, which holds the plug together.

When the clotting factors arrive on the scene, they assist in the formation of a chain of proteins called **fibrin**. The strands of fibrin form a net of tough fibers around the platelets, holding them firmly in place. When someone has hemophilia, one of the clotting factors is missing or doesn't work properly. The blood clot that forms is soft and can easily fall apart. This makes it difficult to stop the bleeding.

THE TYPES OF HEMOPHILIA

There are several different types of hemophilia. Each type is caused by the lack of a specific factor.

Type A is caused by a lack of factor VIII. This is the most common type of hemophilia, affecting 85 percent of those with the disease. It is also called **classic hemophilia**.

Type B is caused by a lack of factor IX. Hemophilia type B is sometimes called Christmas disease, after Stephen Christmas, a Canadian who was the first person diagnosed with this disorder in 1952. About 1 percent of all cases of hemophilia are caused by problems with factors V, VII, X, XI, or XIII.

Hemophilia can be mild, moderate, or severe, depending on the amount of blood-clotting factor a patient produces. People with as little as 10 percent of the normal level of clotting factor may only have serious bleeding

Breakthrough

An anti-hemophilia globulin contained in **plasma** is found to decrease clotting time in patients with hemophilia by Harvard physicians Arthur Patek and F. H. L. Taylor in 1937.

problems after medical procedures such as surgery or after a severe injury. Excessive bleeding after these events may be the first sign that someone has hemophilia.

Severe hemophilia occurs when a person has less than 1 percent of the normal level of clotting factor. In these cases, spontaneous bleeding (bleeding that occurs for no identifiable reason) can result from the ordinary wear and tear of everyday activities. People with severe hemophilia can suffer spontaneous bleeding several times a month if they do not undergo preventive treatment.

GENETICS AND DNA

The majority of bleeding disorders are hereditary. Genetic information is transmitted from parents to offspring via **chromosomes** found in the nuclei (central cores) of cells. Chromosomes are structures made up of proteins and **deoxyribonucleic acid** (DNA). Genes are sequences of DNA located at specific places on a chromosome. Genes act as blueprints for the production of proteins, which are the main substances that make up our bodies. A gene or combination of genes code for a specific trait, such as eye color or a clotting factor.

Almost every cell in your body contains two copies of each chromosome. One of the copies comes from your mother, and one comes from your father. Sperm and egg cells, however, contain only one copy of each chromosome. Sperm and egg cells are formed by a process called **meiosis**. In this process, the pairs of chromosomes are copied and then lined up at different ends of the cell's nucleus. The cell then divides twice to form four cells. In this way, sperm and egg cells are formed that each

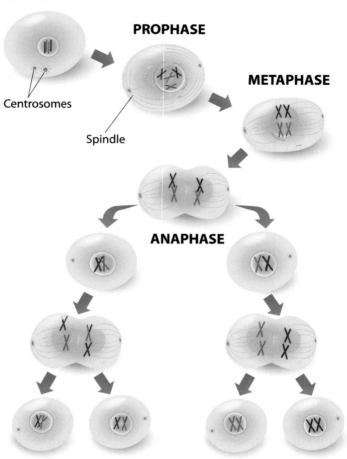

INTERPHASE

PROPHASE

METAPHASE

Centrosomes

Spindle

ANAPHASE

In meiosis (sexual cell reproduction), all chromosomes and a centrosome are duplicated (interphase), the chromosomes pair up and spindles form from the centrosomes (prophase), the nuclear membrane disappears and the chromosomes attached to spindles start to pull apart (metaphase), and the chromosomes move to separate poles and two cells are formed (anaphase). The process repeats except for the duplication of chromosomes, creating four cells, each of which has half the chromosomes of the original.

contain one-half of each chromosome pair. The sperm and egg cells later join, and an **embryo** is formed. The embryo receives one-half of each pair of its chromosomes from its mother and one-half from its father.

Sometimes one of the genes that makes up a chromosome has an error in its sequence, which causes it to work incorrectly or not at all. In the case of hemophilia, this can result in the body not producing one of the clotting factors. This type of error in a gene is usually inherited from a parent who already has the mistake. Sometimes, though, the change is a **mutation**, or a spontaneous change that occurs when the chromosomes are copied during meiosis or early development of the embryo. Scientists estimate that about two-thirds of all new cases of hemophilia are the result of an inherited genetic defect. The other one-third come from new mutations in a gene.

X MARKS THE SPOT

Hemophilia is much more common in boys than in girls. This is because the gene for hemophilia is located on the X chromosome, which is one of the chromosomes that determines the sex of a baby. Females have two X chromosomes. Males have one X chromosome and one Y chromosome. Children get an X chromosome from their mother and an X or Y chromosome from their father. The gene for hemophilia is what is known as an **X-linked recessive gene**. Since a male has only one X chromosome, if his X chromosome contains a defective gene for one of the clotting factors, he will have hemophilia. In contrast, even if a female gets an X chromosome from one parent that contains a defective gene for one of the clotting factors, if she gets a healthy gene for that factor on the X chromosome she receives from the other parent, she will not get hemophilia.

A female with one normal X chromosome and one X chromosome containing the defective gene is called a carrier.

Slower Recovery

The most common bleeding disorder is von Willebrand's disease (VWD). It strikes 1 percent of the US population, so it occurs one hundred times more often than hemophilia. It is an **autosomal dominant disease**. These diseases are transmitted if a child receives an abnormal gene from just one parent. VWD is not exclusively linked to the X chromosome, so it can be inherited from the mother or the father. This is why it affects men and women equally.

This disease is named after Erik von Willebrand, the Finnish doctor who discovered it in the 1920s, and it is closely related to hemophilia. In von Willebrand's disease, a clotting factor known as the von Willebrand factor (VWF) is either insufficient (type 1), defective (type 2), or absent (type 3). This protein circulates with factor VIII, and it is needed for platelets to adhere to blood vessels. This is necessary for clotting, and without it the time when bleeding occurs is longer.

VWF is crucial for stopping bleeding of the skin or mucous membranes. These membranes are found in the linings of the nose, mouth, intestines, uterus, and vagina. Bleeding in those areas is common in people with VWD. This is different than in people with hemophilia. Factors VIII and IX are necessary for stopping bleeding in deep tissues, so hemophiliacs suffer more from bleeding in their muscles and joints.

Parents

Father	Mother
without hemophilia	a carrier for hemophilia gene
XY	XX

Children

Son	Daughter	Son	Daughter
without hemophilia	a carrier for hemophilia gene	with hemophilia	not a carrier of hemophilia gene
XY	XX	XY	XX

Hemophilia is an X-linked recessive disorder. This schematic shows the possible sex chromosome combinations a child could receive from a father without hemophilia and a mother who is a carrier for the condition. Only a male child could get the disease in this scenario, barring a mutation.

Carriers of hemophilia sometimes have other bleeding-related problems, even though they do not have hemophilia. They may bleed more than normal from menstruation, surgery, or nosebleeds. Each time a carrier becomes pregnant, her child has a 50 percent chance of inheriting the defective gene. Any of her sons who receive the defective gene will have hemophilia. Her daughters will not have the disease if they get a normal gene from their father. A female can inherit hemophilia if she gets defective genes from both her mother and father. This is extremely rare.

Factor Factories

Factor VIII is produced primarily by cells in the liver, although some is also made by cells in the kidneys, lymphatic (immune) system, and other locations. Normally, factor VIII lasts for about twelve hours before it is broken down in the body. Von Willebrand factor circulates in the blood along with factor VIII to keep it from breaking down too soon. Von Willebrand factor also helps concentrate factor VIII at sites where damage has occurred. Factor IX, which is defective in hemophilia type B, is also made in the liver. It requires vitamin K to function and lasts about twenty-four hours in the body.

Vitamin K is a group of compounds. The most important of them are probably K1 and K2. The first of these comes from eating herbs, leafy greens, and salad vegetables such as green onion. The second is found mostly in meats, cheeses, and eggs. Deficiencies in K2 are more common than in K1. While a deficiency in vitamin K might lead to bleeding problems, such a deficiency is not usually a result of genetics and is therefore not directly related to hemophilia.

The Royal Disease

Hemophilia came to be known as the "royal disease" because of the way it struck the family of Queen Victoria of England and then was passed on to some of the other ruling families of Europe. The queen tried to cover up the fact that it ran through her bloodline to save her family from shame. Ultimately, the fame of hemophilia's royal victims spurred a great deal of valuable medical research.

Hemophilia isn't always an inherited condition. In the case of the English royal family, it occurred as the result of a random mutation, or change, in a gene. We know this because there was no history of hemophilia in Queen Victoria's family when she came to the English throne in 1837. However, in 1853, the Queen gave birth to her eighth child, Leopold, and he had hemophilia. Since there was no prior history of hemophilia in

Hemophilia showed up in Britain's royal family when Queen Victoria (*seated, center*) gave birth to Leopold (*seated at right in the front row*). Alexandra stands behind the queen.

Victoria's family, a spontaneous change must have occurred in the gene that came from the queen.

Leopold was diagnosed with the disease in 1858 or 1859. He appeared weak and clumsy, bruised easily, and suffered from epileptic seizures. His physician was Sir William Jenner. Jenner had gained his reputation in 1849 by confirming there was a difference between typhus and typhoid fever—thought to be the same disease at the time—and their sources. He found that fleas carried typhus and that dirty water carried typhoid. This information helped public health officials prevent the spread of those two fevers.

Jenner was appointed physician extraordinary to Queen Victoria in 1862. He looked after Leopold from 1861 until the prince's death. During this time he was involved in hemophilia research. He studied the joint tissue of hemophiliacs under a microscope, the second doctor to do so, and in 1876 he reported the fact that the blood of hemophiliacs was slow to coagulate. Jenner couldn't figure out if hemophilia was hereditary. In some families, the disease could be traced for generations. In others, such as the royal family, there was no history of the disease. He didn't solve this riddle.

Prince Leopold's condition was not entirely covered up—an article that appeared in 1868 in the *British Medical Journal* referred to Leopold's serious bleeding problems. In 1884, Leopold was living in Cannes, in the South of France, because it was believed a warmer climate would be better for his health. On March 29 of that year, Leopold suffered bleeding in his brain after a fall and died at the age of thirty.

Leopold was the only one of Queen Victoria's sons to get hemophilia, but two of her daughters, Alice and Beatrice, were carriers of the hemophilia gene. Two of Beatrice's three sons inherited hemophilia. Beatrice also had a daughter, Eugenia, who was a carrier. In 1906, Eugenia married King Alfonso of Spain. Their eldest son, Alfonso, and their youngest son, Gonzalo, both had hemophilia. In the 1930s, they both died of wounds received in auto accidents, complicated by their hemophilia.

Queen Victoria's daughter Alice married Prince Henry of Prussia, part of modern-day Germany. The prince was her first cousin, and their two sons, Waldemar and Henry, both had hemophilia. Waldemar bled to death at age four. His brother Henry lived until age fifty-six.

Leopold died at age thirty after striking his head in a fall.

Out of deference to his family's wishes, details of Leopold's condition were kept out of his obituaries, but the prince's death still brought a lot of attention to the disease. In the 1880s there was a great increase in scholarly articles published about it. These articles were hardly the first to be written on hemophilia, however.

Early Observations

Abu al-Qasim al-Zahrawi, also known as Albucasis, was a famous Muslim doctor born in the tenth century in Córdoba, Spain. He invented a number of surgical instruments, wrote a thirty-volume medical encyclopedia, and was thought by many to be the most important physician in the Middle Ages. One entry in his encyclopedia described a family in which the men

Hemophilia Fact Sheet

» Hemophilia occurs when a person is missing or deficient in a protein needed for blood clotting. The two main forms are hemophilia A (factor VIII deficiency) and hemophilia B (factor IX deficiency).

» Hemophilia A is about four times as common as hemophilia B.

» Hemophilia A occurs in one in five thousand live male births.

» The number of people with hemophilia in the United States is estimated to be about twenty thousand. The worldwide incidence is estimated at more than four hundred thousand.

» There is no cure for hemophilia, but there are very effective treatments available in the United States.

» Hemophilia is usually diagnosed when a person is very young. The median age for diagnosis is one month for people afflicted with severe hemophilia, eight months for those with a moderate case, and thirty-six months for people with a mild case.

» One-third of babies born with hemophilia come from families with no known history of the condition.

Earnest Board's painting *Albucasis Blistering a Patient in Cordova* shows the great Muslim doctor at work.

died of prolonged bleeding from minor wounds. This is believed to be the first detailed description of hemophilia ever recorded.

The first modern description of the disease was made by Dr. G. W. C. Consbruch of Germany in 1793. A few years later, scientific investigation into the disease was stimulated by John Conrad Otto, a doctor living in Philadelphia, Pennsylvania. He published an article in 1803 entitled "An Account of an Haemorrhagic Disposition Existing in Certain Families." "Haemorrhage" means to bleed uncontrollably (although today it is usually spelled "hemorrhage"). In this article, Otto traced the inheritance of hemophilia back through three generations of a family. He demonstrated that the disorder afflicted men in multiple generations, indicating that there was a genetic link.

The term "hemophilia" was used in print for the first time in 1828 by Friedrich Hopff, a medical student at the University of Zurich in Switzerland. He wrote a paper entitled "Uber die Haemophilie oder die erbliche Anlage zu tödlichen Blutungen."

The title translates from German as "On Hemophilia or Hereditary Fatal Bleeding." This work described inherited bleeding disorders that only affected men. He noted that the disease was passed on by women who didn't suffer from the disease themselves. From that time on, "hemophilia" was used to refer to the disease. The word combines the Latin terms *hem*, which means "blood," and *philia*, which means "love" or "attraction." Thus, hemophilia literally means "love of blood."

Breakthrough

British hematologist Robert Macfarlane describes the clotting process in a 1964 paper and names the interaction of clotting factors as the **coagulation cascade**. Today it is known as the clotting cascade.

CHANGING HISTORY

In the early twentieth century, Russia was ruled by **Czar** Nicholas II. One of Queen Victoria of England's granddaughters, Alix (called Alexandra in Russia), married Nicholas. In 1904, Alexandra gave birth to a son, Alexei Nikolaevich, who had hemophilia. He was the fifth child but only son, so he was first in line to succeed his father as czar. His condition would have a major impact on the course of Russian history.

Alexei (*second from right*) was the only son of Czar Nicholas II of Russia and his wife Alexandra.

At that time, there were very few ways to treat hemophilia, and Alexei suffered from debilitating pain. A Russian monk named Grigory Yefimovich Rasputin seemed to have the ability to ease Alexei's suffering. Alexandra made the monk a member of the royal household. In time, Rasputin came to have great influence over the royal family.

Rasputin was popular with the ordinary people in Russia, who saw him as one of their own who had made good. The aristocrats, however, feared that his influence over the royal family was greater than their own. They expressed their distrust of the monk to the royal family, but because he helped her son, Alexandra refused to have him sent away.

In June 1914, World War I struck Europe, and Russia became involved. Many powerful people began to turn against Czar Nicholas. They felt that many of his decisions were endangering Russia. The aristocrats also worried that Czar Nicholas was allowing Rasputin to influence his decisions in order to keep the monk happy. For example, Nicholas allowed Rasputin to decide which government ministers to hire and fire. On December 30, 1916, the aristocrats lured Rasputin into a trap and killed him. This angered the common Russian people, who felt he had represented their viewpoint to the royal family.

Within a few months of Rasputin's murder, the Russian Social Democratic Workers' Party, also called the Bolsheviks, seized power in Russia. They imprisoned and then, in July 1918, executed Czar Nicholas and his entire family. Many historians feel that Rasputin's presence and death were two of the underlying causes of the revolution. Thus, Alexei's hemophilia helped change the course of life in Russia.

There were rumors that Alexei and a sister, Anastasia, survived the massacre of the royal family, and over the years there were many imposters claiming to be the survivors. The most famous of these was Anna Anderson, whose claim inspired the 1956 movie *Anastasia*. However, the remains of Alexei and a sister were found in 2008 and identified by DNA testing, debunking all the claims of the imposters.

A Daily Struggle

From an early age, most people with hemophilia and other bleeding disorders take special measures to minimize their risk. For instance, a child learning to walk may need to wear padded clothing to avoid injuries from falling or bumping into things. A child with hemophilia may have to avoid contact sports for the same reason.

Kristy Dobson followed a different path than most others with a bleeding disorder, however. Dobson has von Willebrand disease, but she didn't allow it to keep her from becoming a competitive figure skater. She represented Canada at international events before a back injury forced her to retire. While skating, Dobson wasn't immune to the problems that other people with bleeding disorders face. She trained for

Kristy Dobson climbed through the ranks of Canadian figure skating despite the dangers the sport presented to her health.

twenty-five hours a week to remain at an elite skating level, and the physical strain resulted in injuries.

A sprain or a bruise from a fall may clear up in a few days for someone without a bleeding disorder. When Dobson suffered a sprain, it could take weeks or months to fully heal—in an article for the Canadian Hemophilia Society, she wrote that she can injure blood vessels or other tissue, causing internal bleeding, just by bending her arm. In one case, an ankle sprain bled into her joint and became infected. This could have been treated with surgery, but that could have damaged her tendons. After weeks on IV medication, the infection went away. Still, Dobson needed months of rehabilitation before she could get back on the ice.

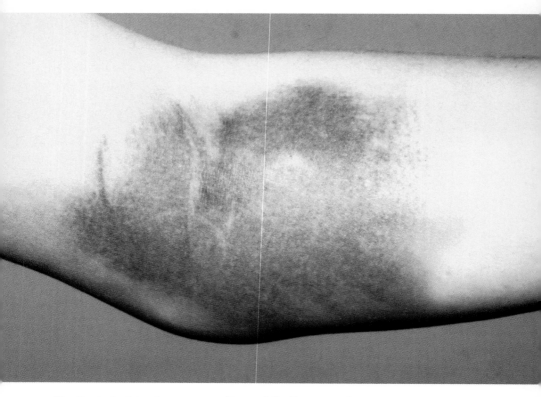

Bleeding in the joints is a symptom of hemophilia. If not treated it can cause permanent damage.

In 1977, Professor Pier Mannucci of the University of Milan in Italy discovered that a compound called desmopressin could be used to treat mild cases of hemophilia type A and von Willebrand's disease. Desmopressin (DDAVP) is a synthetic, or man-made, **hormone**, a compound that affects the way that other compounds or organs in the body behave. Desmopressin increases the release of factor VIII and von Willebrand factor. Dobson kept DDAVP in a refrigerator at home and at the rink, and she taught others how to inject her with it in case of an injury.

"I have had numerous injuries and daily occurrences that have always led me to the hospital for treatment, but I have learned to cope with and overcome my bleeding disorder," the then eighteen-year-old wrote in the 2008 article.

The back injury ended her dream of representing Canada at the Winter Olympics but she is still involved in skating. Dobson has a job with Skate Canada on its High Performance Integrated Support Team.

DISTRESS SIGNALS

The major symptom of hemophilia is uncontrollable bleeding. Sometimes the bleeding is obvious, as in the case of a nosebleed. Sometimes, however, bleeding occurs in the joints or the head and cannot be seen externally. Signs of internal bleeding include a tingling feeling, warmth, or stiffness in the area involved. If not treated promptly, internal bleeding can cause serious damage to the body's joints, muscles, and organs.

A painful headache, drowsiness, or confusion can indicate bleeding in the head. Bleeding in the head is especially dangerous because it can cause brain damage and even death if it is not quickly discovered and stopped. External bleeding is less dangerous and can usually be controlled by first aid.

Trips to the dentist can be hard for people with von Willebrand's disease because their gums bleed easily. Often, they are treated before and during a dental procedure, and for up to five days after.

SIMILAR SYMPTOMS

Many of the symptoms seen in hemophilia can also occur in other types of diseases. If a patient is suspected of having hemophilia, a doctor measures how long it takes the patient's

Bad Blood

Ryan White was three days old when he was diagnosed with hemophilia. He had suffered prolonged bleeding after his circumcision. Like many hemophiliacs in the 1970s, he received weekly blood **transfusions**. At that time, donated blood was not screened. White received blood tainted with Human Immunodeficiency **Virus** (HIV). He was diagnosed with Acquired Immunodeficiency Syndrome (AIDS) when he was thirteen.

Hemophiliac Ryan White contracted HIV during one of his regular blood transfusions.

Hemophilia

People with hemophilia were among the hardest hit groups affected by the AIDS outbreak in the United States in the early 1980s. Up to ninety percent of people with severe hemophilia and, according to the *New York Times*, close to half of all hemophiliacs contracted the life-threatening illness in those early years, and by the spring of 1988, 386 had died from it. HIV caused a severe drop in life expectancy for hemophiliacs until a blood-screening test was invented in 1985 that made receiving transfusions infinitely safer.

White's case became one of the most famous. The school board in his native Kokomo, Indiana, barred him from attending school because he had AIDS. A lawsuit was filed on his behalf in the US District Court in Indiana and he won. He and his mother moved to Cicero, Indiana, where he attended school. He wanted to be treated as just another kid, but that was unrealistic because his fight to go to school attracted international attention. He received a red Mustang convertible from singer Michael Jackson and phone calls from politicians such as Senator Ted Kennedy of Massachusetts and Vice President Dan Quayle, who was also from Indiana.

Ryan White died on April 8, 1990, at the age of eighteen. Among those at his side were his mother and the singer Elton John.

blood to clot and tests for the number of red cells are in the patient's blood—a low number may be a sign of excessive bleeding—and for the presence of specific blood-clotting factors. A DNA test may also be ordered.

Here are the signs of hemophilia:

- » Very large bruises resulting from small accidents that would produce only a small bruise on a healthy person
- » Frequent bleeding from gums, mouth, or nose
- » Bleeding in urine or stool
- » Joint pain and damage as a result of bleeding in a joint
- » Muscle pain as a result of bleeding in muscle tissue that causes pressure on nearby nerves

EARLY TREATMENT

The first approach to treating hemophilia was simply to replace the blood lost with a blood transfusion. In a transfusion, blood flows down a tube into the patient's body through a needle placed in a vein. A transfusion with whole blood (blood that has not been separated into liquid and solid parts) introduces blood-clotting factors that are missing in the hemophiliac's own blood. The first successful treatment of hemophilia by blood transfusion was performed in 1840 by the English physician Samuel Lane.

In 1936, plasma was first used to treat hemophilia. Plasma is the clear, yellowish fluid that is left after the solid blood cells have been removed. It contains elements that cause blood to clot, such as fibrin, but, because the solid blood cells have been removed, it is less likely to cause bad reactions.

As late as the 1950s and 1960s, people suffering from hemophilia were treated with transfusions of whole blood or plasma. Unfortunately, the treatments were often unsuccessful because the transfused blood or plasma did not contain high enough concentrations of clotting factor to stop very serious internal bleeding.

INFUSIONS AND INHIBITORS

A common treatment today for people with hemophilia is to give them **infusions** of clotting factor on a regular basis. This provides protection against uncontrolled bleeding in the event that an injury occurs. However, clotting-factor infusions are not always successful. Sometimes people develop an immunity to the factors. This happens because our immune system is designed to seek out and neutralize foreign particles that get into our bodies. Sometimes when external clotting factors are introduced into a person's blood, the immune system recognizes these elements as foreign particles. The immune system then produces proteins called **antibodies**. The antibodies attach to the clotting factors when they enter the bloodstream, marking them as invaders. Immune system cells then engulf and destroy the clotting factors.

Breakthrough

Freeze-dried, concentrated powders of factor VIII and factor IX become available in the 1970s, allowing hemophilia patients to give themselves infusions at home. This eliminates trips to the hospital.

The antibodies that attach to the clotting factors are called **inhibitors.** They inhibit the action of the clotting factors and make it impossible for them to do their jobs. Most facilities that treat people with hemophilia test for inhibitors. It's also common for their presence to be detected when a patient continues having bleeding problems despite treatment or when patients who previously showed improvement start to bleed again.

If the presence of an inhibitor is suspected, the patient is given a test called a Bethesda assay. The test measures the strength of the inhibitor. The strength of the inhibitor is called its "titer." The titer of inhibitors is measured in Bethesda units, or BUs. A high titer is five BUs or more. Someone with a low titer might respond to treatment with a larger infusion of clotting factor. Those who have a high titer, however, will simply put out more inhibitors to neutralize the clotting factors, and therefore they must rely on other types of treatment.

Those most at risk for developing inhibitors include people of Hispanic or African heritage and those who are younger than twenty years of age. Treatment options for those with inhibitors to human blood-clotting factors include the use of factors that have been altered in a laboratory, or factors that have been derived from pig rather than human blood. The problem with all of these treatments, however, is that they only work in some people. They may also cause dangerous blood clots. Therefore, the appropriate treatment must be determined for each patient on a case-by-case basis.

PROACTIVE TREATMENT

The term **prophylaxis** means taking precautions before a problem starts, which may enable one to avoid the problem altogether. In hemophilia, this term is applied to the regular infusion of clotting factors to prevent bleeding problems before they begin.

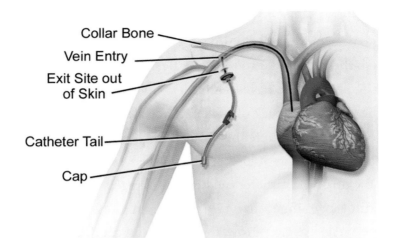

Non-Tunneled Central Venous Access Device

A central venous access device enters the patient near the shoulder and stays in the vein. It allows patients or nurses to perform infusions easily. However, the devices are prone to causing infections and can lead to other difficulties.

Typically, people receive infusions of clotting factor two or three times per week. This helps them keep the level of factors VIII or IX in their blood high enough for clotting to occur. It is common for this treatment to begin when patients are young, often between two and four years old.

Prophylaxis can be a problem because it requires locating a vein for the needle to enter every time an infusion must be given. This is an uncomfortable situation, especially for children whose veins may be hard to locate.

An alternative is the use of a port-a-cath, or central venous access device (CVAD). This device is implanted under the skin either in the upper chest or under the patient's arm. It is left there for a year or more. The device consists of a long, thin tube, or a catheter, that is inserted into a large chest or arm vein, and a reservoir that holds the medication to be supplied. The medication is placed or injected in the reservoir and goes through the tube and into the vein. Because the port is under the skin, people who have them can safely swim or take a bath.

The major drawback of such a device is that patients often develop infections where the device is implanted. The infection rate can be as high as 50 percent in people who have inhibitors. Also, the tip of the catheter can become plugged with a blood clot.

Children younger than two have the highest risk of infection. Also, as they grow, their ports can get displaced and press on veins. Often, the decision to have a port inserted comes down to how close the patient is to a hospital or other health care center. Regular infusions can be given by nurses who are based in a hospital and don't have to travel a long distance. However, people without easy access to such help may choose to have a port inserted so they or a family member can administer infusions at home.

Time of Discovery

Doctor Erik von Willebrand didn't go looking for the medical condition that bears his name. It found him in 1925.

He was asked to examine a young girl from the Åland Islands, off the coast of Finland, who had experienced severe bleeding episodes. The five-year-old, named Hjördis, was one of eleven children, and four of her sisters had died at a young age from uncontrolled bleeding. She had bled from her nose and lips and had to be hospitalized at age three to survive a cut on her lip that bled for days.

After examining her in Helsinki, von Willebrand traveled to the islands to study the disease. He found that twenty-three of sixty-six members of Hjördis's family had bleeding problems. What didn't fit was the fact that more women than men

Dr. James Watson is a Nobel Prize winner who helped discover that DNA is shaped like a double helix.

suffered; it was already known that far more men than women get hemophilia. The doctor wrote about his findings in 1926. Hjördis died of menstrual bleeding at the age of thirteen.

During this time, rapid gains were made in the understanding and treatment of hemophilia and other bleeding disorders. In 1936, scientists discovered that plasma could be used to treat hemophilia. In 1937, two researchers at Harvard Medical School, A. J. Patek and F. H. L. Taylor, discovered that solids removed from plasma, rather than whole plasma, could be injected to make blood clot faster. In 1939, Kenneth Brinkhous at the University of North Carolina demonstrated that people with hemophilia lack a component of the plasma, which he called antihemophilic factor. Today, this substance is known as factor VIII.

In 1944, a doctor in Buenos Aires, Argentina, named Alfredo Pavlovsky found in laboratory tests that blood from one patient with hemophilia could cause the blood of another hemophilia patient to clot. This meant that there were two different clotting factors in the blood (later identified as factors VIII and IX). A patient could lack one but have the other. The same year, Edwin Cohn, an American biochemist at Harvard Medical School, developed a technique for separating plasma into its component parts. This process, called **fractionation**, allowed Cohn and his colleagues to demonstrate that one of the blood fractions, named Cohn Fraction I, contained the blood-clotting factors. Armand Quick, an American doctor, reached the same conclusion that year. The work of these researchers laid the foundation for advances in understanding hemophilia for decades to come.

ADVANCES AND PROBLEMS

In 1955, three American **pathologists**, Kenneth Brinkhous, Robert Langdell, and Robert Wagner, developed the first method of giving patients infusions of factor VIII. Unfortunately, there were problems with this early form of treatment. In the 1950s, plasma from animals such as pigs and cows was used in hemophilia treatments, and many people had serious allergic reactions to these animal products.

In 1957, Inga Marie Nilsson and others at a hospital in Sweden found that the bleeding described by von Willebrand was due to the lack of a plasma factor present in normal and hemophilia A patients. They named the factor after von Willebrand.

In 1964, R. G. Macfarlane identified the process by which various factors work in series to clot blood. In this process, the factors line up like a series of dominoes—when the first one is knocked over, it affects the next, which affects the next, and so on. In the blood, this sequential activation of clotting factors is called the coagulation cascade. Armed with a better understanding of how blood clots were formed, scientists began to search for new ways to treat hemophilia.

COLD FACTS

In the middle of the 1960s, Judith Pool, a doctor working at Stanford University, made a discovery that tremendously advanced hemophilia treatment. She discovered that slowly thawing frozen plasma resulted in the precipitation, or depositing, of solid material at the bottom of a container. Such deposits are called **cryoprecipitates** ("cryo" means frozen). Dr. Pool found that the cryoprecipitates were high in factor VIII. They had much greater power to make blood clot than whole plasma did.

Cryoprecipitates allowed hemophilia patients to treat themselves from home instead of having to travel to a hospital. The cryoprecipitate could be kept frozen at home, and if necessary, a local doctor could perform the infusion after thawing some of the patient's supply of the material. Following Dr. Pool's initial work, researchers at the Plasma

Fractionation Laboratory (PFL) in Oxford, England, produced cryoprecipitates of various other important clotting factors, such as factors VII, XI, and XIII. By 1968, freeze-drying was found to be possible with the cryoprecipitates. This resulted in a powdered form of the clotting factor that could be kept at home and used as necessary.

Dr. Craig Venter (*left*) and Dr. Francis Collins address the media on June 26, 2000, when it was announced that the human genome had been mapped.

DNA AND HEMOPHILIA

The fact that traits could be passed from parents to children was recognized from earliest times. However, it wasn't until the twentieth century that the mechanisms by which this occurred were fully understood. In the first half of the twentieth century, scientists established that DNA was the carrier of genetic information. DNA contains four **nucleotide bases**: adenine (A), thymine (T), cytosine (C), and guanine (G). Genes consist of different combinations of these four bases. In 1953, English scientists James Watson and Francis Crick, along with Maurice Wilkins and Rosalind Franklin, discovered the three-dimensional structure of DNA. They figured out that DNA is a double helix, or two strands twisted around each other in a way that resembles a spiral staircase. Watson later went on to become head of the Human **Genome** Project, whose mission was to map the location of all the genes on human chromosomes.

Breakthrough

Testing for hepatitis C (HCV) in plasma and blood products begins in 1992, all but eliminating the risk of getting the virus during a transfusion. Before testing, an estimated 44 percent of all people with hemophilia contracted HCV.

In order to identify the cause of genetic diseases and treat them, it was necessary to establish the location of each gene, the exact arrangement of bases in it, and the protein it codes for. This was made possible by the invention of techniques for sequencing genes. When scientists sequence genes, they use chemicals to separate the genes into their bases and identify the order in which they occur. In 1977, English researcher Fred Sanger developed the first process for gene sequencing.

In the 1990s, automated methods of sequencing DNA were invented, which made the process of gene sequencing much faster. The Human Genome Project started in the United States

Hemophilia

in 1990. Its goal was to sequence the entire human genome
(a complete set of genes in an organism) by 2005. In 1998,
a competing project was started by Dr. J. Craig Venter with
the goal of sequencing the entire human genome within three
years. They were done by June 2000.

In addition to locating and sequencing genes, a second
set of techniques was necessary to treat a genetic disease like
hemophilia. The goal of these techniques would be to change

In this 2002 photo, Dalton Dawes, an eight-year-old with hemophilia, prepares a $1,000
dose of a medicine administered twice a week.

a "bad" gene into a "good" gene. In the 1970s, two discoveries
took place that made such a transformation possible. In 1970,
a type of protein called a restriction **enzyme** was discovered. A
restriction enzyme can cut strands of DNA at specific points,

Advancements in Hemophilia

- **1793**   The first modern description of hemophilia is made by Dr. G. W. C. Consbruch of Germany.

- **1828**   The term "hemophilia" is used in print for the first time by Friedrich Hopff, a German medical student.

- **1840**   The first successful treatment of hemophilia by blood transfusion is performed by English physician Samuel Lane.

- **1936**   Plasma is first used to treat hemophilia.

- **1939**   Kenneth Brinkhous at the University of North Carolina demonstrates that people with hemophilia lack factor VIII.

- **1955**   American pathologists Kenneth Brinkhous, Robert Langdell, and Robert Wagner develop the first method of giving patients infusions of factor VIII.

- **1964**   English physician R. G. Macfarlane identifies the coagulation cascade.

- **Mid 1960s**   Judith Pool of Stanford University develops cryoprecipitates, simplifying the treatment of hemophilia.

- **1980s**   Methods using heat and chemical processing are developed that inactivate viruses such as HIV, making the clotting factor derived from plasma safer to use.

1984	The gene for factor VIII is isolated and sequenced, making genetic-based treatments for hemophilia possible.
1992	Wyeth, a pharmaceutical company, succeeds in creating the first recombinant clotting factor.
1995	Prophylaxis is made the standard for treatment of bleeding disorders.
1997	The Genetics Institute and Wyeth develop a human protein–free concentrate of recombinant factor IX, called BeneFIX, which can be used to treat hemophilia B.
1998	First human gene therapy trials begin.
2000s	FDA approves first recombinant factor products made without human or animal plasma derivatives.
2009	RiaSTAP is approved by the FDA to treat factor I deficiency.
2011	FDA approves Corifact to treat factor XIII deficiency. It is used for routine prophylactic treatment and to control bleeding before, during, and after surgery.
2013	Gene therapy trials are under way at three sites in the US.

allowing it to be used to "cut out" a bad gene or a portion of it. Then, in 1973, American scientists Stanley N. Cohen and Herbert W. Boyer developed methods of inserting new DNA into a strand of DNA that has been cut by a restriction enzyme. This new combination of genetic material is called **recombinant DNA**.

LOCATING THE GENE

In 1984, the gene for factor VIII was discovered by Jane Gitschier and colleagues at the Genentech company in San Francisco, California. Identification of the gene for factor VIII made genetic-based treatments for hemophilia possible, including infusions of what are known as recombinant clotting factors. In 1992, Wyeth, a pharmaceutical company, created the first recombinant version of clotting factor VIII. This factor, called rAHF (recombinant antihemophilic factor) was developed for the treatment of hemophilia type A. It is produced by inserting the gene for clotting factor VIII into animal cells, such as those from Chinese hamster ovaries. The cells then multiply and begin to produce the clotting factor, which is collected. The factor produced in this fashion is the same, biochemically, as that extracted from human plasma. However, because it does not come from human blood, it is less likely to contain impurities such as viruses that might infect those who receive it.

In February 1993, a second recombinant factor VIII product, Kogenate, was developed. Early recombinant factors such as Kogenate use albumin, a human protein, in their manufacture. This can result in contamination of viruses and may cause an allergic reaction in some people. In response to such concerns, the Genetics Institute and Wyeth developed a recombinant factor IX, called BeneFIX, in 1997. This product is used to treat hemophilia type B. It is produced without the use of plasma or albumin and is, therefore, less likely to cause adverse reactions or infection. In 2002, Wyeth began selling ReFacto, an albumin-free form of recombinant factor VIII.

There is also new hope for patients who develop antibodies to factors VIII or IX. Recombinant factor VIIa is being developed as a treatment for patients who have inhibitory antibodies to these factors. There are drawbacks to these types of products, however. They remain active for only a short time, so they must be given frequently. They can cost $100,000 or more per year.

Although all these approaches are a step forward in treatment, they still rely upon replacement of the missing clotting factor. They do not actually cure the underlying problem that causes hemophilia.

Hope for Gene Therapy

Gene therapy has been held out as the key to curing genetic diseases such as hemophilia. However, since the first gene therapy trials in 1998, there have been many setbacks, and some of them have discouraged people from funding more research.

An early setback came in 1999, when a patient named Jesse Gelsinger died in the United States during a gene therapy trial. Soon after, another damaging case arose in Europe involving children with a form of severe combined immunodeficiency, which is caused by a genetic defect on the X chromosome. This defect prevents people from developing some of the cells that fight off infections. The children were given corrective genes that were packed into modified retroviruses. No one can control exactly where these retroviral **vectors**—a vector is a carrier; a viral vector carries DNA into a host cell—insert themselves.

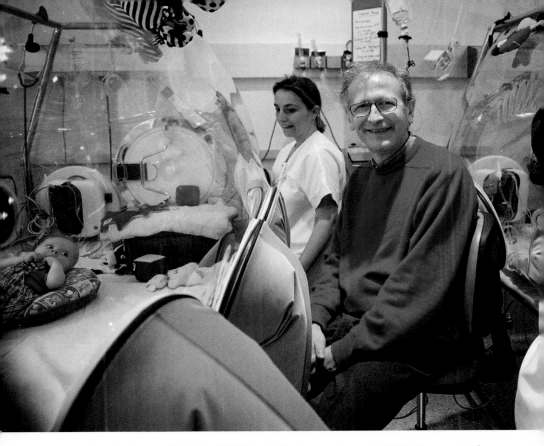

Dr. Alain Fischer cured bubble child Wilco (*left*) with gene therapy in 2002. However, trials ended when other children developed leukemia.

It was thought that if a vector worked on a gene that regulates cell growth and division, cancer could result.

Even though eighteen of the twenty children in the experiment were cured, five of them developed leukemia and one of them died in 2002. Further trials were put on hold.

Another American death in 2007 caused the FDA to stop twenty-eight trials across the country. However, different ways were tried to get new genes into cells without causing cancer, and by 2009 three small successes were reported. In one, ten people with a rare immunological disorder were treated, and eight were cured.

Being Prepared

You may not know her face, but you are probably familiar with her voice. Alex Borstein is a comedian who is the voice of Lois Griffin on *Family Guy*. She is also the National Hemophilia Foundation's spokesperson for genetic testing. Borstein is a carrier for hemophilia A—her factor levels are low and she experiences long, heavy menstrual periods—and she has a brother with hemophilia.

She said she developed her sense of humor through trying to keep the mood light while the family dealt with her brother's condition. She would joke with him as he received his infusions.

Before having children, she and her husband, actor Jackson Douglas, asked other families what life was like with a child with hemophilia. During both of her pregnancies, they had their children genetically tested. Neither one has hemophilia, but she still supports testing for known carriers.

"I want to encourage families to be prepared," she said in an interview for the National Hemophilia Foundation's magazine, *Hemaware*. "If you can arm and prepare yourself, those are the responsible things to do."

Host Alex Borstein (*left*) was joined in 2013 by Marcus Monroe and Sarah Silverman at a hemophilia fundraiser called "What's So Bloody Funny?"

Since then, scientists have found safer vectors and now monitor where the gene lands in the genome. In 2014, the Hemophilia Foundation of American wrote in a press release that "A new technique that uses a class of viruses known as adeno-associated viruses to carry proteins in the body has helped revive interest in gene therapy, which promises long-lasting relief from hard-to-treat diseases by targeting the root cause—bad genes—instead of only the symptoms."

A pharmaceutical company pledged $252 million to a Boston biotechnology company to fund development of a treatment to repair the faulty gene that causes hemophilia A. The hope is that this one-dose therapy will last for years. This will greatly improve the quality of life for hemophiliacs, who for twenty years had to receive injections two to three times a week.

In the spring of 2014, the Food and Drug Administration approved two new drugs, one for hemophilia A and one for hemophilia B, which would allow patients to go five days between injections. This is a good interim step for patients until the gene therapy trials are completed.

Repairing a Gene

Another approach being investigated by researchers involves fixing a gene so that it produces the protein it should be producing. Sometimes hemophilia, as well as many other genetic disorders, results from a mutation in a gene's sequence that stops the gene from making a protein, such as a clotting factor. There was hope that a drug being developed by PTC Therapeutics, known as PTC124, could be used on several diseases.

In 2005, PTC124 was approved by the US Food and Drug Administration (FDA) for use in clinical trials for treating muscular dystrophy and cystic fibrosis. Trials have produced mixed results, with one study saying the treatment doesn't work as claimed. Work on this method continues.

Genetic engineers are looking to modify recombinant clotting factors. One such approach aims to delete the part of the factor that allows it to be broken down, or degraded, in the body. If the factor is not degraded, it will remain active in the body for longer periods of time.

Another area being explored is how to reduce the effect of inhibitors. Research is being directed at creating a hybrid factor VIII **molecule** that is produced by combining human and pig gene sequences. It is hoped that the majority of inhibitory antibodies will bind to one portion of the hybrid factor, leaving the other free to act. We are likely to see the development of other recombinant clotting factors that contain fewer of those sequences that produce inhibitors.

Breakthrough

Prophylaxis becomes common by 1995. This allows children receiving infusions two to three times a week to live with less pain and without orthopedic damage. New products introduced in the 2000s may reduce the frequency of infusions to once a week or less.

HEALTH DEVICES

Dr. Harvey Pollard and his colleagues at the Uniformed Services University School of Medicine in Bethesda, Maryland are

Cloned pigs are used in research seeking ways to reduce the effect of inhibitors in hemophilia patients.

investigating a new, innovative approach. They built thumb-sized devices that were implanted in monkeys and guinea pigs. These were able to continually convert the inactive form of factor VII into its active form, VIIa. Factor VIIa causes the coagulation cascade to happen and eliminates the need to use either clotting factor derived from blood or genetically engineered factor VIII or IX. These implants got around the problem of antibodies attacking protein infusions of factor VIII and making them inactive. This problem occurs in 15 percent of patients who receive the infusions.

Another experimental approach to increase the amount of clotting factor in blood involves the use of microspheres. These are hollow spheres less than 0.0001 inches (0.00254 millimeters) in diameter. These tiny spheres can carry genes into cells or proteins in the bloodstream. Experiments with rats have shown that genes carried by microspheres that are fed to the animals can find their way into cells. This opens up the possibility of their use as a nonviral delivery method for gene therapy. In addition, the researchers demonstrated that proteins can be released into the bloodstream from the microspheres. This creates the possibility of delivering clotting factor in an oral rather than injected form.

One key in the treatment of hemophilia is that the disease doesn't have to be cured for great progress to be made. If gene therapy can help a person go from producing 1 percent of the clotting factor to 5 percent, it will give them a less severe form of the disease, which can be a profound benefit to their lifestyle.

GLOSSARY

antibody • A chemical compound produced by the immune system that attaches to a foreign particle, marking it for destruction by immune system cells.

autosomal dominant disease • A disease someone gets if they inherit the gene for it from only one parent. An autosomal disease is not carried on either the X or the Y chromosome, which determine the sex of the child.

base • In biochemistry, a segment of DNA. The four bases are adenine, cytosine, guanine, and thymine.

chromosome • A long thread of DNA found in the nucleus of cells that consists of a series of genes.

classic hemophilia • Another name for hemophilia type A.

clotting factors • Substances in blood plasma that are needed for clotting to occur.

coagulation cascade • The process by which clotting factors work in series, with each affecting the next one to form a blood clot. Also known as the clotting cascade.

cryoprecipitate • Solid material separated from plasma by a freezing and thawing process.

czar • A king or emperor, usually referring to one of the former rulers of Russia.

deoxyribonucleic acid (DNA) • The chemical compound that makes up chromosomes.

embryo • An unborn human in the early stages of development.

enzyme • A substance that causes a chemical reaction in the body.

fibrin • A chain of proteins that holds a blood clot in place.

fractionation • The process in which a compound such as plasma is separated into its component parts.

gene • A segment of a chromosome that contains genetic information for a particular protein. A single gene—or a combination of genes—determines a trait, such as eye or hair color.

genome • The entire collection of genes of an organism.

hormone • A chemical in the body that affects the way that other compounds or organs in the body behave.

infusion • A solution introduced into the body through a needle inserted into a vein.

inhibitor • A substance that stops a chemical reaction. In hemophilia, inhibitors are antibodies in our immune system that attack blood factors from infusions, keeping them from working.

meiosis • The process that results in the formation of sperm and egg cells.

molecule • A tiny particle consisting of two or more atoms held together by chemical bonds.

mutation • Damage or change in a gene that causes the gene to function differently.

nucleotide • The basic unit of DNA.

pathologist • A physician who studies the causes of diseases.

plasma • The clear, yellowish fluid that remains when the solid blood cells are removed from blood.

platelets • Cell fragments that clump together to form a blood clot.

prophylaxis • Taking precautions to prevent a problem, such as a sickness, from occurring.

protein • A type of substance found in all living things. Proteins are essential to the structure and function of cells.

rabbi • A spiritual and religious leader of people of the Jewish faith.

recombinant DNA • A manmade strand of DNA composed of DNA from different sources.

transfusion • The transfer of blood from one person to another.

vector • A vehicle used to deliver a gene in gene therapy.

virus • A strand of DNA surrounded by a protective shell. A virus attaches to a cell and inserts its DNA into it, taking over the cell's internal components and producing more copies of itself. Eventually, the cell bursts, and the newly created virus particles attach to other cells in the body and repeat the process.

X-linked recessive gene • Usually, a gene is recessive if the trait it codes for is expressed only when a child inherits the gene from both parents. An X-linked recessive gene occurs only on the X chromosome. For female children, who have two X chromosomes, the gene must be inherited from both parents to be expressed. For male children, who only have one X chromosome, an inherited X-linked recessive gene will be expressed no matter what.

Websites

Hemaware

www.hemaware.org

This online magazine of the National Hemophilia Foundation provides up-to-date information about bleeding disorders and how to deal with their associated problems.

Hemophilia Federation of America

www.hemophiliafed.org

Get the latest news about hemophilia, an updated list of events, and information on how you can help the cause at this comprehensive site.

WebMD

www.webmd.com/a-to-z-guides/understanding-hemophilia-basics

Learn the basics of hemophilia and follow links to frequently asked questions and other topics.

Organizations

Canadian Hemophilia Society

301–666 Sherbrooke Street West
Montreal, QC H3A 1E7
Canada
(800) 668-2686
www.hemophilia.ca

National Hemophilia Foundation

7 Penn Plaza, Suite 1204
New York, NY 10001
(212) 328-3700
www.hemophilia.org

FOR FURTHER READING

Ballard, Carol. *Heart and Blood: Injury, Illness, and Health*. Chicago, IL: Heinemann, 2003.

D'Ambrosio, Cheryl Nineff. *Pooling Blood: A Journey of Two Girls With Hemophilia and Their Parents' Struggle to Keep Them Alive*. Bloomington, IN: iUniverse, 2010.

Lewis, Ricki. *The Forever Fix: Gene Therapy and the Boy Who Saved It*. New York: St. Martin's Griffin, 2013.

Mooney, Carla. *Genetics: Breaking the Code of Your DNA*. White River Junction, VT: Nomad Press, 2014.

Panno, Joseph. *Gene Therapy: Treatments and Cures for Genetic Diseases*. New York: Facts on File, 2010.

Potts, D. M., and W. T. W. Potts. *Queen Victoria's Gene: Haemophilia and the Royal Family*. Shroud, England: Sutton, 1999.

Resnik, Susan. *Blood Saga: Hemophilia, AIDS, and the Survival of a Community*. Berkeley, CA: University of California Press, 1999.

Sheen, Barbara, and Beverly Britton. *Hemophilia*. San Diego, CA: Lucent Books, 2003.

Willett, Edward. *Hemophilia*. Berkeley Heights, NJ: Enslow, 2001.

Publications

Burke, Michael G. "Gene Therapy for Hemophilia A." *Contemporary Pediatrics* 18, no. 8 (August 2001): p. 135.

Flieger, Ken. "Outlook Brighter for Youngsters with Hemophilia." *FDA Consumer* 27, no. 6 (July/August 1993): p. 19.

Roth, David A., Nicholas E. Tawa Jr., Joanne M. O'Brien, Douglas A. Treco, and Richard F. Selden. "Nonviral Transfer of the Gene Encoding Coagulation Factor VIII in Patients with Severe Hemophilia A." *New England Journal of Medicine* 344, no. 23 (June 7, 2001): pp. 1735–1742.

Online Articles

Aronova-Tiuntseva, Yelena, and Clyde Freeman Herreid. "Hemophilia: 'The Royal Disease.'" National Center for Case Study Teaching in Science. Accessed May 27, 2015. sciencecases.lib.buffalo.edu/cs/collection/detail.asp?case_id=634&id=634.

Borchers, Callum. "Drug Giant, Startup Seal a Pact Worth Millions." *The Boston Globe*, June 23, 2014. Accessed May 27, 2015. www.bostonglobe.com/business/2014/06/22/dimension-therapeutics-inks-big-pact-with-bayer/pnkCrtp0E8wW7XZtcqUGkI/story.html.

Dobson, Kristy. "How a Bleeding Disorder Has Affected My Life." Canadian Hemophilia Society. Accessed April 4, 2015. www.hemophilia.ca/en/our-stories/kristy---how-a-bleeding-disorder-has-affected-my-life.

DUJS. "A Royal Shame: Prince Leopold's Hemophilia and Its Affect on Medical Research." *Dartmouth Undergraduate Journal of Science*. May 22, 2009. Accessed April 5, 2015. dujs.dartmouth.edu/spring-2009/a-royal-shame-prince-leopold's-hemophilia-and-its-effect-on-medical-research#.VTaHHt7qKJV.

Kolata, Gina. "Hemophilia and AIDS: Silent Suffering." *The New York Times*. May 16, 1988. Accessed April 5, 2015. www.nytimes.com/1988/05/16/us/hemophilia-and-aids-silent-suffering.html.

INDEX

Page numbers in **boldface** are illustrations. Entries in **boldface** are glossary terms.

AIDS, 30–31
Albucasis, 20, **22**
antibody, 33, 47, 53–54
    See also inhibitor
autosomal dominant disease, 14

base, 42
Borstein, Alex, 50, **51**

central venous access device, 35–36, **35**
chromosome, 11–14, **12**, **15**, 42, 48
circumcision, 7–8, **8**, 30
classic hemophilia, 10
    See also hemophilia type A
clotting factors, 4, 9–11, **9**, 13, 23, 32–35, 39–41, 44–45, 47, 50, 52, 54–55
    factor VIII, 10, 14, 16, 21, 28, 33, 35, 39–40, 44–46, 54

factor IX, 10, 14 16, 21, 33, 35, 39
    recombinant factors, 45–47, 53–54
    von Willebrand's factor, **9**, 14, 16, 28, 40
coagulation cascade, 23, 40, 44, 54
cryoprecipitate, 40–41, 44
czar, 23, **24**, 25

DNA, 11, 42–43, 46, 48
    sequencing, 42–43
    structure of, **38**, 42
    testing, 25, 32
    See also genome; recombinant DNA
Dobson, Kristy, 26–29, **27**

embryo, 12–13
enzyme, 43, 46

fibrin, **9**, 10, 32
fractionation, 39, 41
    See also cryoprecipitate